The French Revolution, 1789–94

HODDER HISTORY

MARTYN WHITTOCK

Hodder & Stoughton

A MEMBER OF THE HODDER HEADLINE GROUP

Acknowledgements

Pour Helen et David, Don et Phyllis pour vous remercier de l'amitié et l'hospitalité, et des inoubliables rencontres sur la plage.

The front cover shows 'The Tennis Court Oath' (1789), by J-L. David, and a portrait of Maximilien de Robespierre reproduced courtesy of Photothèque des Musées de la Ville de Paris.

The publishers would like to thank the following individuals, institutions and companies for permission to reproduce copyright illustrations in this book:

AKG Photo London pages 9, 17, 20-21, 27, 29 (top), 37 (top), 42 (bottom left and right), 43 (top); Artwork designed by Anet Meyer/Second Harvest Food Bank of Orange County page 15 (bottom); Bibliotheque Nationale de France page 22 (bottom); The British Library pages 37 (bottom); The British Museum page 41 (DG 9427); Corbis pages 3 (top right), 6, 19, 22 (top); Photothèque des Musees de la Ville de Paris pages 3 (bottom), 15 (top), 16, 23, 29 (bottom), 33, 34, 35, 38, 39 (top), 42 (top left), 43 (bottom).

The publishers would also like to thank the following for permission to reproduce material in this book:
Definition on page 4 reproduced from the *Collins Shorter Contemporary Dictionary*, 1972, with kind permission of HarperCollins Publishers; David Higham Associates Limited for the extracts from *The French Revolution* by Christopher Hibbert, Penguin, 1982; Linda Kelly for the extracts from *Women of the French Revolution* by Linda Kelly, Hamish Hamilton, 1987; Extracts from *Citizens: A Chronicle of the French Revolution* by Simon Schama, Viking, 1989, copyright © Simon Schama, 1989, reproduced by permission of Penguin Books Ltd.

Every effort has been made to trace and acknowledge ownership of copyright. The publishers will be glad to make suitable arrangements with any copyright holders whom it has not been possible to contact.

Orders: please contact Bookpoint Ltd, 130 Milton Park, Abingdon, Oxon OX14 4SB. Telephone: (44) 01235 827720, Fax: (44) 01235 400454. Lines are open from 9.00 – 6.00, Monday to Saturday, with a 24 hour message answering service. Email address: orders@bookpoint.co.uk

British Library Cataloguing in Publication Data
A catalogue record for this title is available from The British Library

ISBN 0 340 78950 6

First published 2001
Impression number   10 9 8 7 6 5 4 3 2 1
Year   2005 2004 2003 2002 2001

Copyright © 2001 Martyn Whittock

Typeset by Liz Rowe
Printed in Italy for Hodder & Stoughton Educational,
a division of Hodder Headline Plc, 338 Euston Road, London
NW1 3BH by Printer Trento

Contents

1 WHAT IS A REVOLUTION?

THIS CHAPTER ASKS

What does the word 'revolution' mean?
How do historians recognise a 'revolution'?

NEW WORDS

ECONOMY: the way work is done and wealth is made and distributed.
POLITICS: how power is used to control and rule a country.
SOCIETY: the way a country is organised. Peoples beliefs, ways of life and ideas.

THE PEOPLE ARE REVOLTING!

Some of the great events that historians study are called 'revolutions'. Historians sometimes called the English Civil Wars, the 'English Revolution'. This ended with the killing of King Charles I in 1649. The Americans had a revolution in 1776. They broke away from being ruled by the British king, George III. This was in the American War of Independence. Then there is the Russian Revolution. In 1917, the ruler of Russia, Tsar Nicholas II, was overthrown. As a result Russia became a communist country until 1990. And, of course, there is the French Revolution. In fact it was the French Revolution which first started people using the word 'revolution' to describe such great events. But what is a 'revolution'?

The word revolution comes from a Latin word meaning to 'turn'.

We talked about revolutions in science. It's like when the wheel of a bike turns right round. It's completed one revolution. But what's that got to do with history?

TURNING, TURNING …

Historians use the word 'revolution' to describe a great turning round in the way a country is run. It is an event (or events) which puts an end to one way of life, or way of ruling a country, and replaces it with another.

Sometimes historians use it to mean a great change in a country's **economy** and **society** over a longer period of time. They call the 18th-century changes in farming the 'Agricultural Revolution'. They call the coming of machines and factories in the 18th and 19th centuries the 'Industrial Revolution'.

Usually, though, the word means a sudden and violent overthrowing of the rulers of a country and great changes in the way a country is run. These revolutions are about **politics**. Politics is about power and who controls power in a country.

SOURCE A

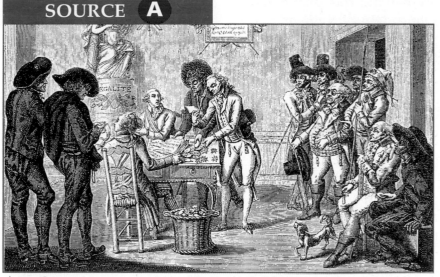

▲ Before the Revolution rich French landowners, called aristocrats, had the power to make villagers work on their lands for nothing and pay taxes to them. During the Revolution many lost their lands and big houses.

SOURCE C

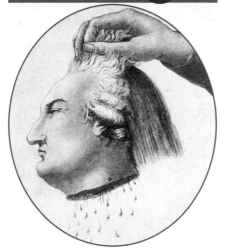

▲ Before the Revolution, King Louis XVI had the final say about how France was run. In 1793 he was executed.

SOURCE B

▲ Before the Revolution members of the Church had a lot of power. In 1792 crowds of workers in Paris slaughtered priests and nuns. Others lost their privileges, wealth and power.

Q

1. Use the word 'revolution' in a sentence explaining what historians mean by this word.

2. Look at **Sources A–C**. Design two posters. Make one a 'Before Poster', showing things about life in France before the Revolution. Then make one an 'After Poster', to show how the Revolution changed France.

Discussion Point

Britain is a democracy. Explain reasons why being a democracy makes it less likely a country will face a revolution.

How unequal was France?

In the French Revolution many of the 'privileged' people in society were overthown. 'Privilege' is when somebody enjoys power, wealth, influence and the 'good things' in life that are denied to other people.

A DIVIDED WORLD

Today most of us living in Western Europe are 'privileged' compared to people in some other parts of the world. Most of us have comfortable houses, a lot of clothes, plenty of food and the latest technology. Yet in other parts of the same world babies starve, **refugees** live in tents, poor farmers struggle to survive. We are privileged.

FRANCE IN THE 18TH CENTURY: THE KING

A small number of privileged people enjoyed most of the wealth and power. This old way of running France is called the '*Ancien Régime*'. At the top was the king. He was an 'Absolute **Monarch**'. He believed he had been given power by God and did not have to share it with anyone else.

THE FIRST ESTATE

Under the king was what was called the 'First Estate'. This was the Roman Catholic Church. It was very powerful. Priests, monks and nuns made up just 0.3% of the population but the Catholic Church owned 10% of the land. Many priests, though, were poor and got on well with their neighbours. Most of the wealth of the Church was enjoyed by a small group of powerful **archbishops**, **bishops** and **abbots**. Small farmers, or peasants, had to pay a tenth (tithe) of all they earned to the Church. Many resented this.

THE SECOND ESTATE

Next was the Second Estate. These were **aristocrats**. They made up only 1.5% of the population but owned 20% of the land. They paid no taxes. They had power over the peasants in the countryside, making them pay taxes, work on the lord's land, pay to use the lord's mill and many other controls that were hated by ordinary people. This Feudal System, which gave them this control over their villages, had died out in England in the Middle Ages! It had not died out in France. Country people hated it. They wanted more freedom. They wanted to be better off.

THE THIRD ESTATE

Everyone else, over 25 million people, were members of what was called the 'Third Estate'. These included everyone from well off middle class doctors and lawyers down to poor peasants. One thing they all had in common was that they had no say in the running of the country.

NEW WORDS

ABBOT: person in charge of a monastery.
ARCHBISHOP: Church leader. Head of a number of bishops.
ARISTOCRATS: rich, noble landowners such as dukes and counts.
BISHOP: Church leader. In charge of the Church in an area of the country.
MONARCH: a king or queen.
REFUGEE: a homeless person escaping from some problem like war or a natural disaster.

SOURCE A

Privilege: a special right or favour, *as Senior pupils sometimes have privileges*.

▲ Collins Shorter Contemporary Dictionary, 1972.

SOURCE B

If the French Revolution was the greatest middle class revolution ever, it owes it both to the stubborness of the aristocracy, which remained firmly attached to its feudal privileges and rejected all changes, and to the passionate opposition of most people to any kind of privilege.

▲ *Written by the French historian, Albert Soboul, in* **The French Revolution, 1787–1799, *1962.***

Absolute King, Louis XVI. His unpopular wife, Marie-Antoinette.

Aristocrats owned rich houses, paid no tax, commanded the army.

Catholic Church controlled education, made peasants pay tithes, it paid no taxes.

Court of the King lived well.

Government of the King able to imprison people without trial using *'lettres de cachet'*.

The Ancien Régime.

The army crushed rebellions.

The part-time soldiers of the *gardes-françaises* kept order.

Peasants, the majority of the population, paid tithes to Church, many taxes to aristocrats and the King. Many peasants owned little land.

Peasants forced to work for nothing on lands of aristocrats.
Middle class had no say in running country.

'The abuses which we must wipe out for the common good are of the widest extent, enjoy the greatest protection, have the deepest roots and the most spreading branches.'

Charles-Alexandre de Calonne, February 1787.

Q

1. What kinds of privileges did the following people have in 18th-century France: the King, the First Estate, the Second Estate?

2. Look at **Source B**. Why, according to this historian, did the French Revolution eventually cause such great changes.

3. You are a French peasant in 1789. Design a protest poster, or write a speech, attacking privileges in France. What changes would you demand?

THE BIG PICTURE

THIS CHAPTER ASKS

Why was there a Revolution?
How did the Revolution happen?
Why was the Tennis Court Oath important?
How important was the storming of the Bastille?

NEW WORDS

ESTATES-GENERAL: a great meeting of representatives of the First, Second and Third Estates. It was needed to agree to new taxes. There had not been one since 1614.

LONG-TERM CAUSES ... SHORT-TERM CAUSES ...TRIGGERS ...

In 1789 there was a revolution against the way France was run. From what you have seen so far the reason why this happened seems obvious: *'The French Revolution happened because ordinary people got fed up with the privileges that the King, aristocrats and rich Church leaders had.'* Well, the answer to that is: *'Yes and no!'*

'Yes', it would never have happened without people feeling angry about the unfairness of life in France.

'No', it was not *just* because of this. After all, lots of other 18th-century European countries were run the way France was. In some Eastern European countries life was worse for poor people. But they did not have a revolution.

So, although the unfairnesses made people angry, there had to be other reasons why this anger exploded into a revolution.There had to be other reasons why the *Ancien Régime* was destroyed. Some were things that had been building up for a long time (*long-term causes*); some took place shortly before the revolution (*short-term causes*); some were events that were the 'last straw' and made all the anger explode into revolution (*triggers*).

In the 18th century population went up – more landless peasants and poor workers.

Since 1700 prices went up more than wages.

Harvests (1787,1788) were bad – people were hungry.

War with Britain (1756–63) caused government to run short of money.

1787. Aristocrats refused to help the king by paying him a land tax.

France helped Americans to defeat the British (1778–83). Cost a lot of money. Government could not afford it.

1788. Government so short of money it planned to call a meeting of the Estates General to agree to new taxes.

1788. Church refused to help the king with money.

Louis XVI, king since 1774, was weak and indecisive. Aristocrats tried to control him.

Estates General met in 1789. The king tried to stop the reforms demanded by the Third Estate – led to revolution.

New ideas – the Enlightenment – were challenging the old power and ideas of the Catholic Church and the Absolute Monarch.

Q

1. What caused the French Revolution? Put events under three headings: *Long-term causes, Short-term causes, Triggers.*

2. Now use three colours to shade in the ones that were: *Political, Economic, Religious, Social.*

3. Put all your ideas together now and explain why there was a revolution in France in 1789?

Game, set and match ...

DREAMS OR NIGHTMARES?

On Monday 4 May, 1789, King Louis XVI, his court and all the representatives of the Estates-General sat together in a church service. During the service a bishop preached a **sermon** calling for the king and his court to improve the way France was governed. At the end of the sermon the king smiled in a way that seemed to promise maybe things would change. The problem was, Louis had been asleep through the whole sermon and had not heard a word! But while Louis was sleeping France was waking up. If Louis was not careful, his dreams would become nightmares.

MONEY, MONEY, MONEY ...

The king was short of money. Expensive wars and bad government had cost a lot. In 1776 he sacked his Finance Minister, Turgot, and replaced him with a Swiss banker named Necker. But he borrowed money and made up figures to avoid trying to make the rich pay more taxes. They paid hardly any as it was! By the time he resigned, the government was desperately short of cash.

The new Finance Minister, Calonne, suggested a land tax in which the rich would pay the most. This seemed a fair idea except to the rich! In 1787 a group of aristocrats, the *Assembly of Notables* rejected his idea. Calonne was sacked. Next the idea was rejected by the *Paris Parlement*, a powerful group of judges who claimed the right to agree or disagree with new laws. In 1788 the Church refused to help Louis. The king and his government were in trouble.

THE ESTATES-GENERAL

The only way to get agreement to new taxes was to call a meeting of the Estates-General. Made up of representatives of the three Estates, it had not met since 1614. This was because French kings tried to rule without getting the agreement of the people. Things were about to change.

On Saturday 2 May, three days before its official opening, the Estates-General gathered. There were 1,201 people in total. Of these 291 were aristocrats, 300 were from the Church (**clergy**). The Third Estate had 610. Most of these were middle-aged, middle class lawyers. They wanted change, not a revolution. They were supported by some aristocrats (eg Mirabeau and Lafayette) and some members of the Church (eg Abbé Sieyès).

NOT EXACTLY A GOOD START ...

On Saturday 2 May, the king met all the representatives of the Third Estate. He spoke to no one except one old man to whom he said, 'Good morning, good man'. The rest were not impressed. Was he really going to listen to them?

The king's brother, Charles, Count of Artois, tried to stop the National Assembly by booking the tennis court for a game of tennis! But the National Assembly moved somewhere else.

SOURCE A

What is the Third Estate? – Everything. What has it been up till now? – Nothing.
What does it want to be? – Something.

▲ *Written by the Church leader Abbé Sieyès, 1789. Unlike many more powerful bishops, he wanted changes in France.*

SOURCE B

They have taken over all authority in the kingdom. They have in one stroke become like the parliament of Charles I.

▲ *Written by the Englishman, Arthur Young, who witnessed the Tennis Court Oath in 1789.*

Q

1. How do **Sources A** and **C** show different views of the importance of the Third Estate in 1789?

2. From what you know about what happened to Charles I in England, what do you think Arthur Young meant in **Source B**?

3. Why was the Tennis Court Oath so important?

Mention: how the *Ancien Régime* was run, how much power the Third Estate had before 1789, how the oath could change France.

THE DEMANDS OF THE THIRD ESTATE

It was the members of the Third Estate who made the revolution. This was not surprising: they paid the most taxes but had no say in the running of the country. They demanded:

- The return of Necker as Finance Minister because they thought he could sort out the money problems.
- A constitution. This was a set of rules which would limit the power of the king and give the Third Estate a say in running the country.
- The Third Estate should speak for the whole country as it represented about 98% of the population.

THE TENNIS COURT OATH

The king would not accept their demands. On 17 June the Third Estate changed its name to the *National Assembly*. A large number of clergy came and joined them.

The next day Louis – on the advice of Queen Marie-Antoinette his wife – shut them out of their meeting place. So they went off to a nearby indoor tennis court. There they swore an **oath** that they would stay together until the king agreed to a constitution. Only one member refused to swear the oath. It became known as the *Tennis Court Oath*. Although they did not know it at the time it was the start of the French Revolution and the end of the *Ancien Régime*.

SOURCE C

▲ *The opening of the Estates-General, 5 May 1789. Clergy on the left, aristocrats on the right, Third Estate at the back furthest from the king.*

A picture paints a thousand words

YOUR MISSION: to discover what messages about the importance of the Tennis Court Oath there are in the painting by Jacques-Louis David.

The most famous picture of the Tennis Court Oath was made by the French painter, David, in 1791. It was first put on display as a drawing and later turned into a full painting by other artists.

David went on to become a member of the *Convention*, (which replaced the National Assembly in September, 1792). He was responsible for abolishing the Academy of Art in 1793. He had always resented it because they only let him join on his fourth attempt. He died in Brussels in 1825.

The person who suggested meeting in the tennis court was Dr Guillotin. He later invented the way of executing people that is named after him.

INVESTIGATION

You are the investigator!

David's painting is full of meanings. Match up each lettered point to the messages.

- Wind of freedom blows.
- Light of truth shines into the room.
- Outstretched arms stand for determination, justice.
- Hands on heart show sincerity, honesty.
- Umbrella inside out stands for society turned upside down.
- Large numbers of people are part of the event.
- A man writing shows new ideas.
- Different parts of the Christian Church united.

Now explain what David was trying to say about the Tennis Court Oath and its importance.

The fall of the Bastille, 14 July 1789

YOUR MISSION: to find out why the people of Paris attacked the fortress of the Bastille.

Middle class members of the Third Estate had forced the King to recognise them as a National Assembly. Perhaps France would reform gradually? But for most French people nothing had changed. In July, 1789, the anger of poorer people in Paris burst into violence. What had started as an attempt to limit the power of the king was quickly turning into a real revolution that would destroy the *Ancien Régime*. On 14 July a crowd of 60,000 people attacked the King's fortress prison of the Bastille in Paris. For many people this was the moment when the revolt of the middle class became the revolution of the ordinary people of Paris.

Why did this happen? What happened? Many people at the time had their own answers. Looking back, historians have not always found the evidence to be so simple. Look at two versions of the storming of the Bastille.

How many people in Paris in 1789 saw it ...

What was the Bastille?
❶ *Hated prison of a hated king.*
Many prisoners kept in chains.

Why was it attacked?
❷ *The king was going to crush Paris with foreign soldiers.*

What happened?
❸ *Seized guns and cannons from Les Invalides. But little gunpowder to fire them!*
❹ *Demanded surrender of Bastille.*
❺ *Governor pointed cannons at us. Soldiers fired.*
❻ *We broke into the Bastille. Many killed.*
❼ *Captured the governor and executed him.*
❽ *Freed many poor prisoners.*

The crowd who attacked the Bastille made anyone around join them in the attack. They even grabbed two British people, who were sightseeing and gave them guns!

INVESTIGATION

You are the investigator!

1. Write two accounts of the attack on the Bastille. One as if you had been there in the crowd in July, 1789. One as an historian looking back. Mention: what the Bastille was, why it was attacked, how the attack was carried out.

2. Why might the accounts not always agree?

Discussion Point

'People living at the time of great events never understand them as well as those looking back.'
Do you agree, or disagree, with this statement?

How many historians see it ...

What was the Bastille?

❶ A prison for enemies of the king arrested without trial, by orders called *lettres de cachet*.
Usually only about ten prisoners.
None kept in dungeons.

❷ Food quite good.

❸ Gunpowder stored there for guns/cannons.

❹ King was bringing soldiers to Paris because of riots. People were afraid.
Bread prices going up.

What happened?

❺ Crowd took weapons from king's store at Les Invalides. Soldiers would not stop them.

❻ Governor of Bastille tried hard to avoid trouble. Crowd attacked Bastille. Some shot.

❼ Governor opened gates – surrendered.

❽ Crowd murdered him, cut off his head.

❾ Freed seven prisoners.

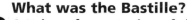

How is the Bastille remembered?

YOUR MISSION: to discover ways in which people since 1789 have remembered the storming of the Bastille. What ideas have there been about its meaning and importance?

NEW WORDS

RESIDED: lived, belonged.
SYMBOL: a sign, or event which stands for something.

We have seen that historians do not agree with the view of people at the time about what actually happened at the storming of the Bastille on 14 July 1789. But how was the storming of the Bastille remembered afterwards? What have people since then thought about it and its meaning and importance? Look at the evidence and decide.

SOURCE A

Bastille Day is the **symbol** of the end of the monarchy and the beginning of the Republic. It was proof that power no longer resided in the king or in God but in the people. The storming of the Bastille symbolises for all citizens of France, liberty, democracy, and the struggle against all forms of oppression.

▲ *From the French Prime Minister's website, AD2000.*

SOURCE B

In the ruined dungeons were still to be seen stones on which had lain the unfortunate prisoners, doomed to die, forgotten by the world, condemned to be buried alive.

▲ *A British tourist explaining what his French guides showed him when he visited Paris in 1790.*

SOURCE C

▲ *A later painting of the storming of the Bastille. It shows far more people involved than do drawings done soon afterwards by people who were there.*

SOURCE D

In 1790 bones found in the foundations of the Bastille were proclaimed to be those of prisoners locked up and forgotten. In fact they were probably those of guards dating from the 15th century.

◀ *An imaginary painting produced some time after the storming of the Bastille. It has been done as a horror painting, showing prisoners chained and rotting away.*

SOURCE E

▲ *A Californian running event, in 1999, aimed to raise money to fight world hunger. The idea is that poverty needs attacking, as it is the oppression that is destroying people's lives today.*

INVESTIGATION

You are the investigator!

Look at the evidence. How has the storming of the Bastille been remembered? What meanings have been given to it?

■ Think about what people thought of it soon after the event.

■ Think about what the French government feels about it today.

■ Think about how some people outside France feel about it.

Discussion Point

What would you describe as the three greatest events that have made our country what it is today?

THE BIG PICTURE

THIS CHAPTER ASKS

How did the Revolution change after July 1789?
Why did it change?
Why did attitudes towards the royal family change?
Why was there war in 1792?

NEW WORDS

APARTMENTS: living rooms.
TRICOLOUR: a badge or flag made up of three different colours.

WHEN WAS THE REVOLUTION?

There were three stages in the outbreak of the French Revolution:

- The revolt of the nobles, 1787–89. When they refused to agree to the king's new taxes.

- The revolt of the middle class, May–June 1789. When the lawyers of the Third Estate swore the Tennis Court Oath and formed the National Assembly.

- The revolt of the people, July–October 1789.

THE REVOLT OF THE PEOPLE

In July 1789 things turned violent. The poorer working people of Paris attacked the Bastille on 14 July. As the news spread, so did the violence. In towns all over France, middle class people formed National Guards to defend the Revolution and their rights. Their badges were red, blue and white. This **tricolour** soon became one of the signs of the Revolution. Red and blue were colours of Paris, white was the colour of the king's royal flag.

The badge of the Revolution was originally the colour green. A revolutionary leader named Desmoulins told the crowd to wear green before attacking the Bastille. Green stood for life and hope. This was changed because it was the favourite colour of the king's brother, Charles.

The National Guard commander, Lafayette, had fought for the Americans against Britain. Although an aristocrat, he was one of the ninety aristocrats in the Estates-General of 1789 in favour of reform.

In the countryside rumours spread, (known as the 'Great Fear') that the king and the aristocrats were planning to destroy the Revolution. Armed peasants attacked the houses of rich landlords. They destroyed the records which said how much the poor owed to the rich. At the town of Agde, the bishop was made to stop taking money from people using the local mill. At Caen, an army officer was murdered when he tried to stop soldiers wearing revolutionary badges.

SOURCE A

▲ *In August 1789 the new National Guard swore oaths to defend the Revolution.*

WHY DID THIS HAPPEN?

There was so much unhappiness with how France was run that, as soon as the king's weakness became obvious, people took the opportunity to attack their rich enemies. The king could not count on the loyalty of his army and so could not stop the disaster happening.

THE REVOLUTION GROWS

Many aristocrats offered to give up their rights. They hoped that this would calm down the attacks on the rich. On 4 August in the National Assembly aristocrats and Church leaders gave up their rights to control the people living on their lands. It was the end of feudalism in France.

A NEW KIND OF FRANCE

On 26 August the National Assembly voted for the *Declaration of the Rights of Man*. This said that all men were equal and had rights to freedom and protection by the law. The king's power was reduced.

The Assembly also said people could keep their property and the poorest people would not get the vote. This was because middle class people were afraid that the poor would want to share out their wealth.

THE MARCH OF THE WOMEN

The king made it clear he did not like the Declaration of the Rights of Man and the end of feudal power. Rumours reached Paris of a feast at Versailles where soldiers had torn off their tricolour badges and the National Assembly had been insulted. On top of this the price of bread was still going up, so that workers were spending half their wages on it. All of this caused anger in Paris.

On 5 October great crowds of poorer women marched to Versailles to demand bread. With them were men determined to bring the king to Paris, to control him.

At Versailles they invaded the National Assembly, and that evening were joined by members of the National Guard who had forced their leader, Lafayette, to lead them to Versailles. That night a group of women and some men burst into the royal **apartments** killing the guards. Marie-Antoinette escaped, wearing only her underclothes. The royal family were forced to return to Paris.

1. Why is it difficult to decide exactly when the French Revolution started?

2. How much had France changed by the end of October 1789? Mention:

- The 'Great Fear'.
- End of feudal rights.
- Declaration of the Rights of Man.
- March of the women to Versailles.

Conclude by saying how great these changes were.

▲ *A drawing of the march of the women to Versailles, made soon after it .*

THE KING OF THE FRENCH …

With the king and the royal family in Paris, the National Assembly, now called the Constituent Assembly, began the job of really changing France. None of its members wanted to get rid of the king. They wanted a **constitutional monarchy**, like Britain. One group, led by Mirabeau, were happy to allow Louis some power. However, another group led by Sieyès succeeded in reducing his power. In 1791 a Constitution was decided which reduced the king's power and changed his title to 'King of the French'. It set up a new ruling group called the Legislative Assembly, whose **deputies** were elected by better off French men.

CHANGING FRANCE

During 1791 new systems of elected local government called *Communes* were set up. There were new courts and judges. **Tolls** were abolished. A decimal system of weights and measures was introduced. Earlier, in July 1790 a law, The Civil Constitution of the Clergy, had taken away Church lands and the power of the pope. Priests were to be elected. This split France. In areas such as in the Vendée, there were Catholic revolts. King Louis XVI eventually refused to accept this law. This was the start of a new period of crisis.

THE FLIGHT TO VARENNES

In June 1791 the king and his family tried to escape from Paris to join loyal members of the army at Metz. The plan failed and they were captured at Varennes. Forced to return to Paris through silent and angry crowds, Marie-Antoinette's hair turned white.

WAR

In April 1792 France declared war on Prussia and Austria. They had been helping aristocrats who had fled from France (called *émigrés*). The group of people in the Assembly who pushed for war were called the *Girondins*. The war went badly and it looked as if France would lose.

THE COUNTRY IN DANGER!

Panic swept Paris. Poorer working people, called **sans-culottes** set up the Paris Commune to control the city. Rumours spread that the king was planning to crush the Revolution. On 10 August crowds invaded the palace of the Tuileries, murdering the royal guards. In September gangs of sans culottes invaded Paris prisons and murdered the people there accused of opposing the Revolution. These 'September Massacres' were supposed to remove anyone who might rise up against the Revolution now that France was losing the war. About a thousand defenceless people

So many rich people fled to Britain from France and tried to sell their jewellery that by 1806 one London jeweller employed over a thousand people in his workshops to rework, and sell it.

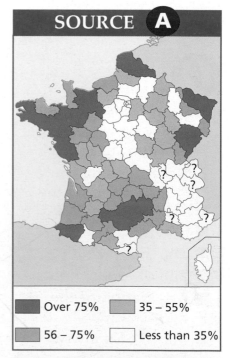

SOURCE A

Over 75%	35 – 55%
56 – 75%	Less than 35%

▲ *Map showing areas of France where priests refused to accept the government taking over the Catholic Church.*

were butchered in horrible ways. One girl was forced to drink human blood to save her father's life.

On 21 September France became a republic. In the elections to the new National Convention all the more moderate and conservative members were defeated. Now the Girondins battled with a more extreme group, called the Jacobins, for who would control France. The Jacobins, supported by the sans-culottes, dominated the Convention.

THE REVOLUTION BECOMES MORE EXTREME

On 20 September the Revolutionary armies defeated the Prussians at Valmy. The Revolution was saved. Unhappy at how violent the Revolution was becoming, Lafayette surrendered himself to the Austrian enemy - who put him in prison for five years! In November the Edict of Fraternity called on all Europeans to overthrow their leaders. In December the king was put on trial. On 21 January 1793 he was guillotined. The crowds dipped their fingers in his blood, one exclaiming 'It tastes horribly salty'. Where would the Revolution go next?

NEW WORDS

CONSTITUTIONAL MONARCH: a king who shares power with an elected group.
DEPUTIES: elected members of a law-making group.
GUILLOTINED: head cut off.
SANS-CULOTTES: poorer Parisians. It means 'without breeches' (the short trousers worn with stockings by the rich).
TOLLS: taxes for travelling through an area.

SOURCE B

▲ *The execution of Louis XVI, 21 January 1793.*

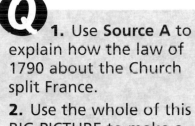 **1.** Use **Source A** to explain how the law of 1790 about the Church split France.

2. Use the whole of this BIG PICTURE to make a timeline of events: 1789–93. Mark on it any 'turning points', events which made great changes to France.

3. How different was France in 1793 compared with 1789? Mention:

■ The monarchy
■ People's rights
■ Church power
■ Feudalism
■ How great were these changes in France?

Why did the Revolution become extreme?

No one who swore the Tennis Court Oath in 1789 could have imagined how France would have changed by January 1793. The Revolution, which at first had very moderate aims, had become violent and extreme. It seemed as if the middle class lawyers and reforming aristocrats like Mirabeau and Lafayette had lost control to the violent Paris workers – the sans-culottes and their friends the Jacobins. By 1793 the Revolution had become very bloody. But what had happened between 1789 and 1793 to cause the Revolution to become so extreme?

The first plan for an international terrorist organisation was made in December 1792. The revolutionary, Marquis de Bry wanted 1,200 men to murder rulers across Europe. It did not happen.

Q **1.** Look at each of the events, or issues. Explain how each might have made the Revolution become more extreme and violent.

2. Which do you think was the most important reason and why?

3. Using these ideas to help you, explain why the Revolution had become so violent by 1793.

Discussion Point

Is it ever right to use violence to achieve political goals?

End of royal authority meant no one could really control France.

King tried to veto (stop) revolutionary laws.

War defeats caused fear of hidden 'enemies'.

Economic problems made sans-culottes call for extreme action against 'rich enemies'.

National Guards fired on rioters in 1791 – angered many sans-culottes, weakened power of Lafayette.

Legislative Assembly could not control sans-culottes.

Foreign Duke of Brunswick (1792) promised destruction of Paris if royal family harmed.

Groups like Jacobins encouraged extreme demands.

Some parts of France refused new laws about Catholic Church – France split.

Emigrés abroad worked against Revolution.

The King must die ...

YOUR MISSION: to edit an edition of the newspaper, Le Père Duchesne, demanding the death of the king.

NEW WORDS

VETO: the King's power to stop a law he did not like. This angered many revolutionaries who felt he was stopping reforms.

Jacques René Hébert ran one of the most extreme newspapers in Revolutionary France. He hated the royal family and used the rudest language to describe them. He called Marie-Antoinette 'The Austrian bitch', the 'she-wolf' and claimed she wanted to 'roast alive all poor Parisians'. He called Louis XVI 'Monsieur **Veto**, the drunken drip', and the king's sister, Princess Elisabeth, 'Big-arse Babet'. He called on sans-culottes to murder aristocrats. Hébert was leader of the Paris Commune and called being guillotined 'shaking the hot hand'.

In January 1793, his newspaper called for the death of the king. Look at some of the reports that his reporters might have sent him. How might he have used these to put together a front page demanding: *The King Must Die ...* ?

Hébert's *Le Père Duchesne* pretended Marie-Antoinette was terrified when she was guillotined. In fact, she was very brave. But Hébert was terrified, for all to see, when he was guillotined in 1794.

REPORT 1

◄ *Remember how Louis tried to escape, in June 1791, but was caught at Varennes?*

REPORT 2

◄ *Marie-Antoinette is a monster. She is a sex maniac and she makes the king oppose the Revolution. They are one as bad as the other. They are 'one monster with two heads'.*

REPORT 3

▲ The king is a drunk.

REPORT 4

You are a fat pig, whose appetite costs the people 25 millions a year.

▲ Said by a National Guard to Louis in April 1791.

REPORT 5

The Constitution is absurd and detestable.

▲ From a letter written by Louis and found when sans-culottes invaded the Tuileries Palace, in August 1792.

REPORT 6

The king has had warehouses at Verdun and Longwy stuffed full of gold and grain, so our enemies, the Prussians, will capture them ...

▲ Rumours heard around Paris.

REPORT 7

Louis tried to stop the calling of the Estates General in 1789.
He planned to use force against the National Assembly in 1789.
He tried to escape in 1791.
He has secret plans to get his power back.
He has vetoed laws that reform France.

▲ The official charges against Louis at his trial, 1792–93.

INVESTIGATION

You are the investigator!

You are one of Hébert's editors. You have to plan out the front page of *Le Père Duchesne*. As you plan it out look at the reports you have received and then decide:

■ What your headline will be.

■ How you will remind people of things Louis has done in the past to cause you to be angry.

■ What kind of person you think he is.

■ What you think of the queen.

■ Why Louis is, in your opinion, an enemy of the Revolution.

■ What the official charges against him are.

■ Why you think he should die.

4 THE TERROR

THIS CHAPTER ASKS
What was 'the Terror?
What kind of man was Robespierre?

THE ROOTS OF THE TERROR

Between September 1793 and July 1794 France was gripped by a terrible period of killing called the Terror. Why did this happen? The Revolutionary Armies' successes in northern Italy, Belgium and Germany after the battle of Valmy, soon turned to defeats. The cost of living was going up. Food was scarce. There was **civil war** in that part of France called the Vendée, as royalists and Catholics fought the hated Revolutionary Government. The Revolution seemed in danger. There seemed to be enemies everywhere. The group of deputies who controlled the **Convention** – the Girondins – were caught between **counter-revolutionaries** and those wanting the Revolution to go much further. These were the sans-culottes and the *enragés* (wild men) led by Hébert and allied to the Jacobins.

FIGHTING FOR POWER

In March 1793 the Revolutionary Tribunal and Committee of Public Safety were set up to fight enemies of the Revolution. One of the leaders was Danton. A strange looking man, whose face was scarred by being twice attacked by a bull as well as being trampled by a herd of pigs as a child, he was a powerful speaker. But he soon faced demands from the sans-culottes and *enragés* for the arrest of the Girondins.

One of those who demanded this was Marat. Suffering from a terrible skin disease and wearing round his head a cloth soaked in vinegar to ease his terrible headaches, he and the sans-culottes eventually had the Girondins arrested. Now the Jacobins, supported by the sans-culottes and *enragés* were in control of Paris. Danton was thrown off the Committee of Public Safety and replaced by a Jacobin named Robespierre. Robespierre held power in France until 1794.

THE MURDER OF MARAT

In July 1793 Marat was murdered in his bath by a woman named Charlotte Corday. The Committee of Public Safety was now under pressure to slaughter any enemies of the Revolution. In September sans-culottes invaded the Convention, demanding 'terror' against people they said were enemies of the Revolution. Faced with losing control of Paris, the members of the Convention gave way.

> Before he was guillotined, Danton said to the executioner, 'Show my head to the people. It's well worth having a look at!'

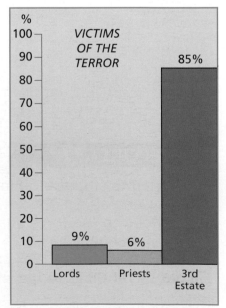

Victims of the Terror chart:
VICTIMS OF THE TERROR
Lords 9%
Priests 6%
3rd Estate 85%

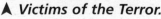

▲ *Victims of the Terror.*

October 1793: Queen Marie Antoinette executed.

October 1793: Girondins executed; many priests executed.

November 1793: Groups of revolutionaries fight for power. Danton calls for end of Terror. Attacked by Hebert.

December 1793: 2000 people executed at Nantes.

March 1794: Hebert and enragé leaders executed.

April 1794: Danton executed.

June 1794: New law speeds up trials; no defence, no witnesses needed. Many innocent people die.

July 1794: Robespierre executed. End of Terror. 3000 had died in Paris, 14,000 across France.

Q

1. Imagine you are a sans-culotte in September 1793. Why might you want a Terror in France? What kinds of people might you think were enemies?

2. Look at the graph. What does this tell you about what the Terror was really like.

3. Using all the information explain:

■ What the Terror was ■ Why it started

■ What happened ■ Why it ended.

Living and dying in the Terror

What was it like to live through the Terror? In one sense it looked as if France was being turned upside down. The Terror was totally destroying the *Ancien Régime* and anyone who opposed change. Everything associated with the old way of life of life seemed under attack. In a Paris park, groups of Parisians abused an old lion that had been brought from the royal animal collection at Versailles. It was, they said as they kicked it, poked it, spat at it, 'a creature of royalty', a 'king of beasts'.

From 1792 a new calendar was introduced. It replaced the old months of the year with twelve new ones, each having thirty days. Weeks were replaced by blocks of ten days. And in 1793 the killing increased as all who stood for the old way of life were destroyed. But what was happening? What was being destroyed? Who was being killed and why? What was it like to live through it all?

NEW WORDS

BLASPHEMY: a rudeness to God.
INDIFFERENT: not caring, not being keen.
LAMENTING: being sad.
TREE OF LIBERTY: tree decorated with the revolutionary colours and badges.

SOURCE A

We must rule by iron those who cannot be ruled by justice. You must punish not merely traitors but the **indifferent** too.

▲ *Spoken by the Jacobin Saint Just.*

SOURCE B

The bishop who prevented a priest from marrying committed a **blasphemy** against the rule of the people. And church towers should be demolished because they are higher than other buildings and so against the idea of equality.

▲ *Accusation against the Church by Delacroix and other anti-Christian Revolutionaries.*

SOURCE C

If we stop too soon we will die. We have not been too severe. Without the Revolutionary Government the republic cannot be made stronger. If it is destroyed now, freedom will end tomorrow.

▲ *The Jacobin, Robespierre defending the Terror in 1794.*

SOURCE D

Sisters were killed for crying over the deaths of their brothers, wives for **lamenting** the fate of their husbands, innocent peasant girls for dancing with the Prussian soldiers.

▲ *Written by the Englishman, William Hazlitt, who based his view on reports he heard from France.*

SOURCE E

A woman was charged with having cried when her husband was executed. She was made to sit several hours under the blade which dropped on her, drop by drop, the blood of her husband, before she was released from this agony by her own death.

▲ *Written shortly after the Terror by the Girondin, Jean-Baptiste Louvet.*

SOURCE F

Jean-Baptiste Henry for cutting down a **Tree of Liberty**.

Jean Julien for shouting 'Long live the King'.

Henriette-Francoise de Marboeuf for having hoped for the arrival of the Prussians.

Francois Bertrand for providing soldiers with sour wine which was bad for their health.

Marie-Angelique Plaisant for saying that she was an aristocrat and did not care 'a fig for the nation'.

▲ *Some of the thousands executed during the Terror, along with their 'crimes'. From a list put together in France shortly after the Terror.*

SOURCE G

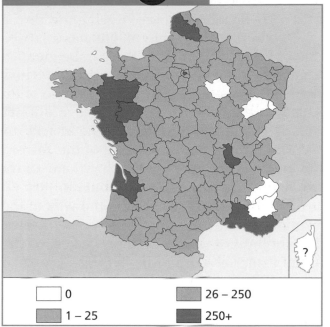

☐ 0		☐ 26 – 250	
☐ 1 – 25		☐ 250+	

▲ *Map showing whereabouts in France victims of the Terror were executed.*

◄ *Picture drawn at the time showing a Section Committee. These gave people certificates stating they were loyal citizens. If they decided not to give a person a certificate, that person's life was in real danger.*

SOURCE H

Q

1. Look at **Sources A–C**. Explain what the Jacobins thought Terror would achieve.

2. a. Do you think Hazlitt (**Source D**) and Louvet (**Source E**) would have agreed with them? Explain your answer by mentioning the way in which these two writers describe the events of the Terror.

b. Hazlitt was English; Louvet was a Girondin. How might this affect how reliable their reports are as evidence?

3. Does **Source F** make you more, or less, likely, to believe what they wrote?

4. Look at this unit and the BIG PICTURE. You are awaiting execution in 1793. Write a letter to a British friend. Explain what it is like in the Terror, how and why people suffer, whether the Terror affects all of France, things people do to try to avoid arrest, why you have been sentenced to death. Perhaps, write in French.

Robespierre and the Terror

WHY DID ROBESPIERRE LEAD A REIGN OF TERROR?

The leader of France during the Terror was Maximilien Robespierre. He was a Jacobin leader and one of those who wanted there to be great changes in France and how it was run. During 1793 he became one of the leading members of the Committee of Public Safety. This was the main group in the Revolutionary government during the Terror. It organised the attacks on 'enemies' of the Revolution. But by the end of the Terror many people hated Robespierre. They felt that many of those killed were not really enemies of France at all. In July 1794 he was overthrown and executed. On the way to the guillotine one woman shouted at him, 'You monster spewed out of hell. The thought of your execution makes me drunk with joy.'

Robespierre was a rather strange, cold man. One man who knew him said he had the look on his face of 'a cat lapping vinegar'. But was he really a bloodthirsty monster? Why did he do the things he did? What did he believe in?

Robespierre was not the first revolutionary to try to change how a country was run. In the 1640s and 1650s Cromwell had tried to change England, during the English Revolution. How does Robespierre compare with Cromwell?

NEW WORDS

BRUTALISED: make cruel and uncaring.
HOARDING: holding on to grain to make it cost more.
PATRIOT: loving your country.
TYRANT: a cruel ruler who has all the power.

SOURCE A

We are all throwing ourselves into each other's arms. The **tyrant** is no more.

▲ *A revolutionary newspaper the day after Robespierre's execution.*

SOURCE B

The bastard isn't satisfied with being the boss. He's got to be God as well.

▲ *Muttered by a sans-culotte at the ceremony in honour of the Supreme Being, 8 June 1794.*

SOURCE C

He saw none of the victims perish. He had once said that public executions **brutalised** people. But he made no move to stop them. He had to stay in power because he thought himself incorruptible, more virtuous than other men. He alone could save the Revolution.

▲ *Historian, C. Hibbert, The French Revolution, 1980.*

A Revolutionary Life ...

1788 Became a lawyer, helping poor people. Attacked royal power and arrests without trial.

1789 Represented the Third Estate in Estates-General.

1790 Became leader of Jacobins, wanting more reforms.

1791 Wanted votes for all adult men. Opposed racial and religious discrimination.

1792 Opposed revolutionary war. Wanted king's death.

1793 Arrested Girondins who opposed reforms giving power and wealth to poorer people. Facing civil war and enemy invasions, Robespierre called for power of a dictator to save the Revolution. Tried to keep Revolutionaries united. Opposed *enragés* who attacked the better off and clergy. Set limits to prices. Used force against people **hoarding** grain. Used Terror against enemies but opposed pointless executions. Opposed slaughters outside Paris.

1794 Opposed attacks on Christianity. Believed in God, tried to create a new religion of the Supreme Being. Moderates *and* extreme people attacked him. Accused of being a dictator. Lost support of people as food remained short. Arrested in July (new name *Thermidor*). Executed.

SOURCE D

His social ideas consisted in reducing extreme inequalities of wealth, in increasing the number of small property owners, and in ensuring work and education for all. He was a man with a sense of duty and of sacrifice.

▲ *Encyclopaedia Britannica.*

SOURCE E

▲ *Drawn in 1794, after his death, this picture is titled, 'Robespierre guillotines the executioner, having guillotined all of France'.*

SOURCE F

▲ *Robespierre plays blind man's buff with death. Drawn after his execution.*

Cromwell: Another Revolutionary Life

1640 As an MP he was against King Charles I trying to rule without agreement of Parliament.

1641 Supported attempts to reduce power of the bishops. Believed Christians could have a direct relationship with God.

1642 Fought in Civil War. Chose men because of what they were like not because they were rich. Brilliant general.

1649 Supported death of the king. Earlier he tried to bring peace with the king but felt Charles could not be trusted.

1653 Felt Parliament would not reform and replaced it with men he thought he could trust. But decided they wanted to make too many changes to the country. He reluctantly replaced them as Lord Protector. As Protector he encouraged education, ended religious persecution, opposed death penalty except for serious crimes. But against reforms that would have given more power to the poor.

1658 Cromwell died.

Q
1. Explain what Robespierre wanted the Revolution to achieve. Look at **A Revolutionary Life** and **Sources** C and D.

2. Why do you think some people, like those in **Sources A, B, E, F** thought as they did? How fair were their opinions?

3. Think of what Robespierre wanted in France and what Cromwell wanted in England. Make a chart to show how they were *Similiar* and *Different*. Then do the same for how they ruled. How alike were they?

5 WHAT DID THE REVOLUTIONARIES WANT?

THIS CHAPTER ASKS
What did the different Revolutionaries want?
How much did they improve the lives of women, black people, working people?

DID ALL THE REVOLUTIONARIES WANT THE SAME THINGS?

The simple answer is 'no'! The different people who made the French Revolution in 1789 did not all want the same things. They had different reasons for being unhappy with the *Ancien Régime*. They had different demands. They had different hopes.

As time went on, it became clear that the different kinds of revolutionaries could not agree. They began to fear each other. The poor felt the middle class had taken over as the rulers of France and were still exploiting them. The middle class feared that the poor would steal their property and cause chaos and violence.

A French historian, Pierre Vergniaud, writing in 1847, said, 'There was reason to fear that the Revolution might devour each one of her children'. When the revolutionaries began to kill each other it was because they wanted such different things from 'their' Revolution.

So many people seemed against the king that, in 1790, Mirabeau said, 'The king has only one man he can count on – his wife.' It also shows how strong and tough people thought Marie-Antoinette was.

DEMAND 1

Gentlemen we are being dictated to in an insulting manner. I demand that you assume your power to make laws. And stick by the oath you have sworn. This means we must not separate until we have made a **constitution**.

▲ *The Comte de Mirabeau, in June 1789, when the king refused the reforms demanded by the Third Estate.*

DEMAND 2

Bread! Bread! Meat at six **sous** a pound! No more talking. We'll cut the queen's pretty throat.

▲ *Chanted by the market women who marched to Versailles in October 1789.*

DEMAND 3

Rents have gone up. The prices of goods have doubled. We cannot afford to live in our own homes. Taxes without number pile on our heads. All we want is our own land on which we can live. But for some time we have not had even this.

▲ *Complaint from the village of Le Montat in 1789.*

Reforming aristocrats and middle class members of the Third Estate.

Declaration of the rights of Man.

Peasants.

Sans-culottes, the working people of Paris.

Q 1. Identify which of the three demands goes with the three different groups of Revolutionaries.

2. Why is is difficult to say what the Revolution demanded?

■ Explain what a 'demand' is.

■ Show how different types of people had different reasons for being unhappy with how France was run.

■ Explain how this led to different demands.

■ Finish by saying why it would be hard for the Revolution to meet everyone's demands. Which group do you think was most likely to get what it wanted? Why?

Discussion Point

How did the English Revolution in the 17th century also lead to people having different hopes about what it would achieve?

Not your usual Revolutionary ...

WHY DID TALLEYRAND SUPPORT THE REVOLUTION?

When we think of the French Revolution we tend to think of the middle class members of the Third Estate, or the sans-culottes storming the Bastille. But many of the early leaders of the Revolution were aristocrats and Church leaders who thought that France could be improved by reforms that would not turn it upside down. One of these was Charles Maurice Talleyrand-Périgord. He was Bishop of Autun and a very rich man.

TALLEYRAND – THE SURVIVOR ...

Talleyrand managed to survive right through the Revolution. He was later a leading member of the government under the Emperor Napoleon (see Chapter 6, BIG PICTURE) and continued to be so when France had a king again after 1815. He was a guest at the coronations of four rulers of France: Louis XVI (1774), Napoleon (1804), Charles X (1824), Louis-Philippe (1830).

Eating only one meal a day and described in 1828 as 'death in black silk' by the painter, Scheffer, Talleyrand was not the kind of revolutionary we expect. He was rich and powerful and managed to stay that way! Most of all, he was a survivor. He changed his views to keep alive and in power.

Many people despised him. Napoleon called him 'excrement in a silk stocking'. But what kind of man was Talleyrand? Why did he support the Revolution?

NEW WORDS

ADMINISTRATION: running of a country.
ENLIGHTENMENT: 18th century ideas about how countries should be 'reformed' and 'improved'.
MODERNITY: modern ways of running a country.
REPRESENTATIVES: people elected to make laws.
TRIMMER: someone who changes their views in order to stay on top.

SOURCE A

Talleyrand was a born **trimmer** and survivor.

▲ *The historian, C.Hibbert, The French Revolution, 1980.*

Life of Talleyrand

1779 became a priest (later a bishop).

1785 defended the Church against king.

1789 member of Estates-General. Attacked Church

1796 returned to France. Joined Government.

1799 supported Napoleon taking power.

1814 betrayed Napoleon. Supported return of king.

SOURCE B

Talleyrand gathered round him the businessmen and their supporters, who, for all they gained from the system, would readily abandon it for another which would protect their fortunes.

▲ *The French historian, A.Soboul,* **The French Revolution, 1787–1799,** *1962.*

Talleyrand loved the cheese called Brie. He called it the 'king of cheeses'. One person who knew him said it was the only king to whom he had been loyal!

SOURCE C

Those in favour of modern ideas and a popular monarchy – like Talleyrand – were all produced by the **Enlightenment**. They believed in liberty, progress, science, property and fair **administration**. Their language was reasonable and their tempers cool. What they had in mind was a nation given, through its **representatives**, the power to strip away things blocking **modernity**. Such a country (probably a monarchy) would not wage war on the France of the 1780s but would complete and improve it.

▲ *The historian, S.Schama,* **Citizens,** *1989.*

SOURCE D

▲ *Portrait of Talleyrand, painted by Jean-Baptiste Belliard.*

Q **1.** Look at **Sources A-C**. What reasons do they suggest for Talleyrand supporting the Revolution?

Do you agree with their views on him?

2. Imagine you are Talleyrand. Tell your life in your own words:

■ Your background
■ Why you supported change
■ Whether the Revolution went as you hoped
■ How you managed to survive
■ What you got from the Revolution.

Discussion Point
What do you think would be the characteristics of a really 'good' politician?

1792 ambassador in London.

1794 attacked in France. Fled to USA.

1814 back in royal government.

1838 died, having apologised to the Church.

Revolutionary women

YOUR MISSION: to find out how much the Revolution changed the lives of French women.

NEW WORDS

POPULAR SOCIETIES: clubs to discuss politics.
ROSTRUM: platform from which to make a speech.
SCAFFOLD: execution place.

Women played an important part in the French Revolution. To many revolutionaries, Louis XVI's wife, Queen Marie-Antoinette, was the most hated member of the French royal family. They accused her of the most unbelievable things and she seemed to stand for all the privilege and wrong doing of the rich. Then it was Parisian women who forced the king to move to Paris in October 1789. Other women demanded greater freedom in the future. But what freedoms did French women want? Did they all agree? Did the Revolution deliver these freedoms?

SOURCE A

▲ *A picture drawn in 1789 showing problems faced by women.*

SOURCE B

All female and male citizens must contribute to the making of laws. No one must be stopped from expressing their beliefs. Woman has the right to mount the **scaffold**; she has equally the right to mount the **rostrum**.

▲ *From the* Declaration of the Rights of Women, *by the revolutionary woman, Olympe de Gouges.*

SOURCE C

However gifted women may be in some respects, they should never show their talents in public.

▲ *The supporter of the Girondins, Madam Roland.*

SOURCE D

Anyone who votes against the rights of another, whatever their religion, colour, or sex, has from that moment given up his own rights.

▲ *Written in 1790 by a man in favour of women having the vote, the Marquis de Condorcet.*

SOURCE E

Let us carry weapons. Let us show men we are as brave and good as them. Let us break our chains. Let us return to the days when women debated with men in public meetings and fought beside their husbands against the enemies of freedom.

▲ *Theroigne de Méricourt, a woman Jacobin, in 1792.*

SOURCE F

I had neither the talent nor the experience. And above all I was a woman.

▲ *De Méricourt explaining why her revolutionary club for women – Les Amis de la Loi – failed in 1790.*

SOURCE G

They would far rather come home to find their house cared for than wait for their wives to return from meetings that did not make them sweeter tempered.

▲ *Complaint by Paris working men.*

SOURCE H

Her wish to be an intellectual led her to forget how a woman should behave. This forgetfulness led her to the scaffold.

▲ *Written by a man in the paper,* Moniteur Universel *about the execution of Madam Roland in the Terror, in 1793.*

SOURCE I

Eight months ago we had bread and today we don't. If you complain about it you are arrested. The **popular societies** have been closed. We are slaves again.

▲ *Complaint by working class women in Paris, 1795.*

SOURCE J

Women are not capable of taking part in government or joining political clubs. They are too emotional and uneducated.

▲ *The Jacobin man, André Amar, supporting a law banning women's clubs and meetings, 1793. It followed street battles between different women revolutionaries.*

SOURCE K

▲ *Festival, 1793, to remember the March of the Women to Versailles.*

SOURCE L

By the end of 1793 the ideas of equal education for women had been dismissed. Women's clubs had been shut. The mob, so vital in the early stages of the Revolution, was a threat to the government it had helped bring to power. The question of women's rights was never an important issue for most women at the time.

▲ *Written by the modern historian, Linda Kelly, in 1987.*

INVESTIGATION

You are the investigator!

Do you agree with the historian in **Source L**?

■ Think about what different women wanted.

■ Decide what problems they faced in getting changes.

■ Look at different men's reactions.

■ Decide how much really changed for women.

> Madam Roland was so brave she asked for a fellow prisoner to be guillotined before her, so he would not be frightened by the sight of her death.

The Revolution and Black people

INVESTIGATION

YOUR MISSION: to design a monument to commemorate the life of Toussaint L'Ouverture.

NEW WORDS

CONGRESS: the US parliament.
EMPIRE: where one country conquers other countries and people.
PLANTERS: White owners of land worked by Black African slaves.

The effects of the French Revolution were not only felt in Europe. Far away, in the Caribbean, the island of St Domingue (now called Haiti) was part of the French **Empire**. Here many Black slaves were forced to work on land owned by White French people. When news came of the Revolution many Black slaves rose in revolt. They wanted the same freedom that White French people had said was their right in the *Declaration of the Rights of Man*.

The man who eventually became the leader of this great uprising for freedom was named Toussaint L'Ouverture. Imagine you have been given the job of putting up a monument to commemorate this Black hero of the Revolution. But first you must find out something about him and what he did.

A map showing France and Haiti. ▼

SOURCE A

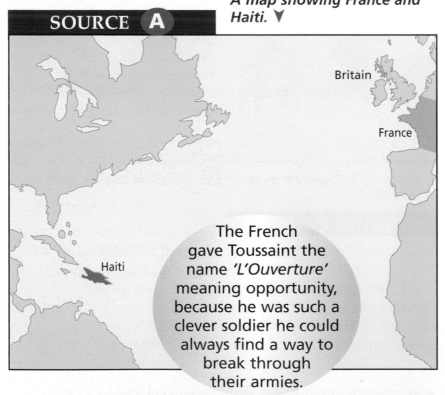

Britain

France

Haiti

The French gave Toussaint the name *'L'Ouverture'* meaning opportunity, because he was such a clever soldier he could always find a way to break through their armies.

SOURCE B

For Black Americans this was a terribly exciting moment. For White American **planters** it was a moment of enormous terror. The American President Jefferson was terrified of what was happening. He accused Toussaint's army of being cannibals. He called on **Congress** to stop trade with Haiti. This destroyed the weak economy of Haiti. And of course Jefferson then said this was what happened when Africans were allowed to rule themselves.

▲ *Professor D.A.Egerton, Le Moyne College, USA, 2000.*

SOURCE C

During peace talks Toussaint was kidnapped by the French and taken to France to be imprisoned until he died in 1803.

▲ *From the website, World African Network, 2000.*

SOURCE D

Toussaint was a good looking man, taller than average, with bold and striking looks, yet polite and educated. He was terrible to an enemy, but kindly to his friends.

▲ *Written by the White British writer, Marcus Rainsford, in* **An Historical Account of the Black Empire in Haiti,** *1805. This description is based on accounts by people who knew Toussaint.*

SOURCE E

Toussaint is a villain. He is a snake which France has warmed against its body.

▲ *French description of Toussaint after he freed Haiti from French rule.*

SOURCE F

The soil ran with blood, dead bodies were heaped one on the other, mangled and mutilated. Toussaint took no part in doing these terrible things. Toussaint has been called harsh. I cannot say that all these accusation are wrong. But it is just as true to say that his enemies have done their most to point out any wrong things in his character. Despite this enough excellence remains to make us admire him. With Toussaint, God was at once the only reality and the supreme good.

▲ *Written in 1853 by the White Rev John Reilly Beard, who carried out much research on Toussaint.*

SOURCE H

▲ *No pictures of Toussaint exist from his life time. This was painted in France in 1832. Some historians think that after 30 years of other people attacking him, the artist was influenced to deliberately give him an 'ape-like profile'–an act of racism.*

SOURCE G

◄ *Toussaint, drawn by a supporter in 1853. It shows the moment when he was tricked by the French and captured.*

INVESTIGATION

You are the investigator!

Decide the words to go on Toussaint's monument.

■ Why was he famous?

■ Why did he act as he did?

■ What impact did he have on other people? Why did some people dislike him?

■ How has he been described by different people in the past and today?

■ What should he look like in any carving on the monument?

■ Why is he remembered as a 'great' man?

What about the workers?

YOUR MISSION: to discover whether the Revolution improved the live of French workers.

On the evening after the Bastille fell, King Louis XVI returned home from hunting. When told about the attack he asked, 'Is this a rebellion?' 'No, Sire', the Grand Master of the Wardrobe replied, 'it is a revolution'.

It was the workers of Paris who really made the French Revolution 'Revolutionary'. They were angry at their lives, angry at the rich and wanted things to change. But what did they want? And how much really changed?

NEW WORDS

CONSTITUTION OF '93: Law of 1793, passed by the Committee of Public Safety, promising the vote to all men, work for the unemployed, support for the sick. It did not happen.
MAXIMUM: law during the Terror controlling prices.

SOURCE A

Vive le Roi, Vive la Nation.

In September 1795 the price of sugar was nearly six times higher than in May. Firewood cost over three times as much as in May. The overall cost of living was about 30 times higher than it had been in 1790.

◀ *Drawn in 1789 this picture shows the hopes of many working people. It says, 'I knew we would get our turn one day'.*

SOURCE B

When the people place themselves in a state of revolt, they take back all power from other authorities and take it on themselves.

▲ *Paris workers in August 1792, the day they set up a Revolutionary Commune to control Paris. The day before they attacked the royal palace of the Tuileries.*

SOURCE D

The Queen is to blame for our starvation. We must march to Versailles and demand bread.

▲ *Spoken by a Paris market woman to the crowd that marched to Versailles in October 1789.*

SOURCE C

To your pikes, good sans-culottes, sharpen them up to exterminate aristocrats.

▲ *Written by the revolutionary, Hébert, 1792. Hébert was a leader of the Paris workers.*

SOURCE E

▲ On Sunday 17 July 1792, thousands of unemployed workers protested about the way the Revolution seemed to be only helping the middle class. The National Guard – made up of middle class people – fired on them and killed 50. Workers called it the 'Massacre on the Champs de Mars'.

SOURCE F

Citizens of every sort are beginning to lose patience with the workers. The National Guard, merchants, manufacturers, craftsmen all say these people are paid by trouble makers. They ought to be swept out of the way by cannon fire.

▲ From the French newspaper, Le Babillard, 6 July 1792.

SOURCE G

We demand bread and the **Constitution of '93**. The people are being starved. Shop keepers are charging high prices. This is the struggle of the black hands against the white.

▲ Demands of Paris workers against the new Directory government in May 1795.

SOURCE H

Absolute equality does not exist. We must be ruled by the best citizens. You will find such men among those who own some property. You must protect the political rights of the well-off and restrict the political rights of men without property.

▲ Speech by Boissy d'Anglas in June 1795. A new law gave the vote only to the better-off.

INVESTIGATION

You are the investigator!

Plan a speech for a Paris workers' protest in 1795.

■ What changes did you expect from the Revolution?

■ Who has opposed you and why?

■ Why are you so angry?

SOURCE I

The government did away with the **maximum** and price controls. That winter (1794–5) workers began once more to look back to the Terror, 'when blood flowed and there was bread'.

▲ The historian, S.Schama, in Citizens, 1989.

6 AN END TO REVOLUTION?

THIS CHAPTER ASKS
How did the way France was ruled change between 1794–99?

What problems did the Revolutionary governments face after the death of Robespierre?

How did Napoleon Bonaparte take power in France?

How did French society change after 1794?

NEW WORDS
COALITION: group of countries working together.
EXILED: made to leave the country.
FAMINE: dying from hunger.

Robespierre was executed on 28 July 1794. In the new French calendar this month was called *Thermidor*. The Terror was over, but what would happen next? Where would the French Revolution go?

A BIT OF THIS AND A BIT OF THAT ...
The men behind the death of Robespierre were the new rich in France. They had gained through buying the land taken from the Church and from émigré aristocrats who had fled abroad. These men tried a political juggling act.

France had only taken control of Corsica in 1768. If it had not, Napoleon would never have become Emperor of France.

We must protect the Revolution. France must stay a republic. The Church and émigrés must not get back their lands.

We must protect ourselves. No more Terror. No equality of wealth and property. Keep the sans-culottes under control and out of power.

CONTROLLING THE REVOLUTION
In 1795 a new constitution was decided:

- Only better-off people could vote.
- Law were made by two chambers (groups) to stop one becoming too powerful.

- Government controlled by five powerful men called the *Directory*.
- Every year elections would choose a third of the lawmakers and one member of the Directory.

THE GOOD AND THE BAD NEWS ...

In some ways things went well for the new rulers. The French army won battles in the Rhineland, Italy and Spain. The Prussians and Spanish made peace with France.

A young Corsican general called Napoleon Bonaparte had great success fighting the Austrians in northern Italy. In 1797 the Austrians had to accept that France controlled large parts of Italy, Belgium and parts of the Rhineland. In 1799 a new **coalition** (against France) of Britain, Russia and Austria broke up because they could not agree.

But in France the economy was in trouble. Prices went up. In 1795 there was **famine** in parts of France. Paper money became worthless in 1796. Poorer people became restless. In May 1795 there was a sans-culotte revolt. The Directory crushed it with the army and took weapons away from the Paris workers. In 1796 more workers wanting wealth shared out more equally had their planned revolt crushed.

The Directory faced attacks from both Jacobins (wanting more change) and Royalists (wanting to restore a king). They were helped by the fact that many people were unhappy with the way the Directory was ruling France. In October 1795 the young General Bonaparte used his cannons to crush a Royalist revolt. He called it 'a whiff of grapeshot'. In 1797 more generals and politicans who wanted to bring back the monarchy were **exiled**.

FROM REPUBLIC TO EMPIRE

The Directory was afraid it would be overthrown. They hoped to use the army to keep it in power. Three of its members asked the popular General Bonaparte for help. In November 1799 Bonaparte used his soldiers to help him (and two members of the Directory) take power. These three *Consuls* now ruled France.

But Bonaparte wanted more. He soon made himself First Consul for life and, in 1804, crowned himself Emperor of France. This was not what the revolutionaries of 1789 had intended!

Napoleon Bonaparte
- **1769** Born in Corsica.
- **1784** Joined French army.
- **1793** Fought Royalists and British at Toulon.
- **1795** Saved Directory; 'whiff of grapeshot'.
- **1796** In charge of army in Italy. Became a hero.
- **1798** Defeated Egyptians. French fleet sunk by British. Abandoned his army, came back to France.
- **1799** Overthrew Directory.

SOURCE A

▲ *British cartoon from the time showing Napoleon (the Crocodile) taking power from the elected lawmakers (shown as frogs) in 1799.*

Q
1. Make a spidergram of the problems faced by the Directory.

2. Beside each problem explain what it did to try to overcome each problem.

3. Imagine you are one of those who swore the Tennis Court Oath in 1789. Explain how you feel about what happened in 1799.

If the cap fits ...

YOUR MISSION: to find out what fashion can tell us about changes in France

Fashions de Paris 1789

Fashions de Paris 1790

Fashions de Paris 1793

People often wear clothes to make statements about themselves. This is nothing new! As France changed, fashion changed. People tried to say different things about themselves and about what they felt about life. Look in the shop windows of Paris from 1789 to 1799. Watch the world of fashion change, as France changes …

Fashion Designer's Notes...

1789 Show how rich you are. Lots of colours, wigs, rich materials.

1790 Dress more simply. Lots of blue, white and red.

1793 Look like a worker. Casual, throw on clothes.

1795 Show you're not a sans-culotte. Show off your money. Long hair, layers of clothes, bright colour. Wigs for women and revealing dresses.

1799 Quietly wealthy. Elegant Greek style for women. Tight and formal for men.

Fashions de Paris 1795

There were parties held in 1794 called *bals des victimes*. These were given by, and for, people who had lost relatives in the Terror. People cut their hair short like that of prisoners to be guillotined. They wore thin bands of red silk around their necks, as if their heads had been cut off.

Fashions de Paris 1799

![I] NVESTIGATION

You are the investigator!

You are a top fashion writer. You have an assignment to write an article for a modern Fashion Magazine, to explain changing French fashions and what these fashions say about life in France. Look at the *Fashion Designer's notes* … Use them and the clothes to write your report. You will also need to check back in this book to see what was going on in France each time and how fashion fitted into these events.

7 WHY WAS THERE A REVOLUTION?

You have looked at the events of the French Revolution.

- The different causes of the Revolution.
- The ways these led to Revolution.
- The events of the Revolution and how the Revolution changed between 1789 and 1794.
- The demands and hopes of different groups. And how far they got what they wanted from the Revolution.
- The ways in which the Revolution had changed by the time the Directory fell in 1799.

PUTTING IT ALL TOGETHER

Now it is time to put it all together. This means answering the two *big questions* that have guided the whole of this exploration: *Why was there a Revolution? How much did the Revolution change France?*

You will need to work on two piece of extended written work to answer these two *big questions*. You could hand write it, or word process it. This is how you could do it:

- For each piece of writing, explain the *big question* you are going to answer.
- Then look at each one of the *little questions*, which help you structure your answer. Each one of those little questions appears in this unit, along with some clues to get you started. Choose the bits of evidence which are relevant to each *big question* you are trying to answer.
- Then finish with a conclusion. This should draw it all together. One piece of written work will end with you saying what you think was the greatest cause of the Revolution. In the second piece of written work, you should say how much France had really changed by 1794, and then by 1799.

What were the causes of the Revolution?

What did the revolutionaries want?

How did the aims of the Revolution change over time?

How much did France change?

Did any lasting good come from the Revolution?

Index